SOARING

SOARING

Phyllis J. Perry

A FIRST BOOK

Franklin Watts

A Division of Grolier Publishing

New York • London • Hong Kong • Sydney

Danbury, Connecticut

Cover design by Wing Chan
Interior design by Janice Noto-Helmers

Photographs ©: Archive Photos: 19; Charles O'Mahony: 8, 9, 23, 25, 26, 28, 29, 31, 34, 35, 36, 37, 38, 39, 41, 43, 44, 46, 47, 50, 52, 55; Comstock: 14, 21; Corbis-Bettmann: 16; Culver Pictures: 12, 18; Jim Daniels: 32, 48; Tony Stone Images: cover, 3, 11 (Tony Hutchings).

Archive Photos: background ghost image of glider throughout

Library of Congress Cataloging-in-Publication Data

Perry, Phyllis Jean.
    Soaring / Phyllis J. Perry.
        p. cm. — (A First book)
    Includes bibliographical references and index.
    ISBN 0-531-20258-5 (lib.bdg.)   0-531-15852-7 (pbk.)
    1. Gliding and soaring—Juvenile literature. I. Title. II. Series.
GV764.P47 1997   96-41075
797.5'5—dc20   CIP
                                                       AC

Contents

CHAPTER ONE

The Thrill of Flight

A bright-blue sky and puffy white clouds make for perfect soaring conditions.

You are 2,000 feet (610 m) above the ground. It's early afternoon on a sunny day with a gentle wind blowing about 10 miles (16 km) an hour. Puffy white clouds are forming in the bright-blue sky. It has been a perfect day for soaring. You glance at the yaw string in front of your canopy, which is streaming straight back. You have been flying in rising air now for more than two hours, catching one thermal after another.

Reluctantly you realize you must stop soaring like the eagles. It's time to descend to earth. But you linger for one last look. Up here, you get a different perspective and a fabulous view of your world. You

Making a final approach

see the airport below. Then, slowly, you sink down, down, down.

Gently, you raise the glider's air brakes by pulling back on a lever in the cockpit. This creates extra drag by disturbing the air that is flowing across the top of the wings. Now you are just 2 feet (61 cm) above the runway. You ease back the stick and touch down, bumping along on your single front landing wheel. A perfect landing! A perfect flight!

Deploying the air brakes (orange panels on wing)

During this flight, you have not been using an engine. Sailplanes climb mostly by riding thermals.

Thermals are created when air is warmed through contact with heated areas on the ground such as roads, buildings, beaches, and plowed fields. When the sun heats up the ground, the heat is transferred to the air just above it, sometimes causing circular air movements referred to as "dust devils." The warming air expands above the heated surface and forms a kind of bubble. When the bubble grows big enough, it floats up like a hot-air balloon. Other bubbles form, and the process is repeated. Soon there is a column of rising warm air—a thermal.

Thermals cool as they rise. Their moisture condenses and forms clouds. When the air is full of thermals, pilots can fly from one thermal to another. If there are only a few thermals, the pilot must turn in circles, called thermaling, to stay within the column of rising air.

The word *sailplaning* and the more common terms *gliding* and *soaring* are used almost interchangeably. The Federal Aviation Administration (FAA) uses the term gliders in its license certificates. Gliding refers to forward and downward movement. Soaring occurs when an aircraft gains altitude through natural lift.

Whichever term is used, soaring is a dream for many people. But it doesn't have to remain a dream. Many young people take lessons. Students as young as age fourteen can earn a glider pilot's license. Although it requires lots of hard work, when you are up soaring in the clouds, you experience a personal satisfaction that makes it all worthwhile.

CHAPTER TWO

The First Gliders

This ancient wood engraving (the first picture ever printed of human flight) records the flight of Daedalus and Icarus.

From earliest times, people have yearned to fly. There are many stories about attempts at flight using wings made out of feathers. One of the most famous legends is that of Daedalus and his son, Icarus, who were held captive on the Greek island of Crete. In this legend, as they try to escape on their hand-crafted wings, the hot sun melts the wax holding the feathers in Icarus's wings, and he falls into the sea.

Another famous story tells of an English monk named Oliver of Malmesbury. The monk is said to have jumped from a tower using homemade wings in 1020. His attempt to fly, however, failed.

Artist and inventor Leonardo da Vinci, who lived from 1452 to 1519, included among his inventions a machine that he called an ornithopter. This air machine resembled a bird's wings in shape and was powered by the rider's leg and arm muscles. But humans were unable to pedal and flap hard enough to lift both themselves and the heavy flying machine into the sky.

It's not surprising that so many early flight experiments were clumsy. These early experimenters did not fully understand the forces that affect the flight of an aircraft: gravity, drag, and lift.

It was in 1804, while experimenting with kites, that a British scientist, Sir George Cayley, discovered that air must be forced over a wing to create lift. With this new understanding, Cayley attached a kite to a long stick, added a movable tail, and put a small

balancing weight at the front. Cayley's kite was the first glider.

The first full-sized glider was built in 1809. The first manned glider flight, however, did not take place until 1853, and the glider crashed after a brief flight.

One famous early glider was flown by a Frenchman named Jean-Marie Le Bris in 1856. Le Bris built the winged contraption, hired a driver with a cart and horse, and stood in his machine on the cart. When the horse was moving at a good clip, Le Bris changed the inclination of his machine's wing and took off. Unfortunately, not only did Le Bris fly but so did the cart driver, who got tangled in the rope.

In 1865, Louis Pierre Mouillard went 138 feet (42 m) using a glider built in Algeria. In these early attempts, people tried to fly by jumping from cliffs and running down hills while attached to their "wings." Their flights were very haphazard. It was not until 1891 that gliders that could be controlled by the pilot were built.

In the 1890s, German engineer Otto Lilienthal conducted many glider experiments during his efforts to build an airplane. He studied bird flight

German engineer Otto Lilienthal made his first glider launch from a man-made hill in 1891.

and tested fixed-wing hang gliders made of wood and fabric. After gathering information from thousands of his hang glider flights, he wrote essays and a book that proved of great help to other experimenters, including the Wright brothers. To fly, Lilienthal would run down a knoll and launch himself into the wind. He was able to glide about $\frac{1}{4}$ mile (400 m). In 1894, Lilienthal built a single-wing glider that became very popular.

In 1903, Matthew Bacon Sellers built a Lilienthal model glider. He found it hard to balance, so he came up with a new design. Experimenting in Warren County, Georgia, he built a staggered quadruplane hang glider in 1905. Each wing was staggered behind and 2 feet (61 cm) below the one above. These machines were called "step gliders."

People continued trying unsuccessfully to find ways to power a flying machine. While early steam engines provided power for movement, they were too heavy and too big to fly. Not until the late 1800s, when gasoline engines were developed, was it finally possible to build a powered flying machine.

The most famous of the early airplane builders were Wilbur and Orville Wright. Their motorized plane, the *Flyer*, flew for twelve seconds on December 17, 1903, at Kitty Hawk in North Carolina. Before building the *Flyer*, however, the Wright brothers built and flew many gliders. They attached control wires to the wingtips so that they

Before their famous motorized flight in 1903, Wilbur and Orville Wright experimented with many gliders.

could turn their glider. They also added a tail with a vertical fin and a fuselage, or body.

Once engine-powered planes were developed, interest in gliders decreased, but it did not die. After the end of World War I in 1918, the victorious Allies, fearing that airplanes might be used in a future war, did not allow Germans to build and fly motorized aircraft. So an estimated 200,000 Germans learned to fly gliders during the 1920s and 1930s.

A breakthrough in soaring occurred in 1929 when two Germans, Alexander Lippisch and Robert

In the 1920s, soaring became a major national sport in Germany.

19

Kronfeld, invented the variometer. This instrument allowed a pilot to know the rate at which the glider was climbing or sinking. Such readings enabled pilots to locate and circle in thermals.

When German glider pilots visited the United States, interest in gliders grew. Three American brothers, Paul, Ernest, and William Schweizer, built many of the first U.S. gliders in Elmira, New York, in 1930.

After the end of World War II in 1945, gliders, or sailplanes, rapidly gained popularity. Some people bought war-surplus training gliders, and before long, factories in America and elsewhere began building sailplanes to fill the demand.

CHAPTER THREE

Drag and Lift

Sailplanes rely on the natural forces of drag and lift to soar.

Powered aircraft usually depend on engines, propellers, jets, or rockets to drive them forward. For sailplanes, or gliders, natural forces act as their "engines." A sailplane produces its own forward motion using gravity. The sailplane gets its forward speed by nosing down and allowing gravity to pull it along.

To understand how sailplanes work, you must know about two things. The first involves the glider wing's design.

The underside of a glider wing is flatter than the top of the wing, which is arched. When the glider is moving, the wing splits the air. The air that moves over the curved top of the wing must travel a greater distance than the air moving along the flatter underside of the wing. The air flowing above the wing must travel faster to catch up with the air flowing underneath, which reduces pressure on top of the wing. Since the pressure underneath the wing is greater, the wing—and the glider—is forced upward. This force is called lift.

The other thing that will help you understand how sailplanes work is called the angle of attack. The angle of attack is the angle at which the wing meets the air. If the nose of the sailplane is pulled too far up, the angle of attack is too steep to allow the air to flow around the top surface of the wing. Instead, the air tumbles around, causing turbulence at the rear top surface of the wing. This turbulence produces a force called drag, which works in opposition to lift.

When drag overpowers lift, the glider is said to be stalled.

When a sailplane stalls, the nose comes down lower than the tail because it is heavier. This new positioning of the nose immediately causes a more favorable angle of attack. With the nose pointed straight ahead or down, and with the wings level, the sailplane will again have lift.

A glider pitches nose down after the pilot has changed its positioning, or angle of attack. This causes the glider to pick up speed rapidly and increase lift.

When a sailplane stalls at low altitudes, it can be very dangerous because there is little time or altitude for the pilot to level out the glider again. A sailplane may also stall if it is moving too slowly.

A sailplane's performance ability is expressed in terms of glide ratio, which is also called lift-to-drag (L/D) ratio. An L/D ratio of 25 to 1, for example, means that the sailplane will travel 25 feet (7.6 m) forward for every foot (30 cm) that it loses in altitude. A high performance sailplane will have an L/D ratio of 30 to 1 or greater. Some of the best competition sailplanes have ratios as high as 50 to 1.

CHAPTER FOUR

From Wing to Wing

The control stick next to the pilot's right hand moves the glider's ailerons, which help turn the aircraft, and the elevator, which helps point the glider's nose up or down. The blue lever controls the air brakes.

A sailplane, or glider, has three basic parts: the wings, the body (or fuselage), and the tail assembly.

A glider's wings are long and narrow. Hinged panels at the rear edge of the wings help turn the sailplane. The panels located at the sailplane's wingtips are called ailerons. The panels located between the fuselage and the ailerons are called flaps. The pilot changes the sailplane's direction and altitude with the glider's control stick and pedals. When the pilot moves the control stick sideways, the glider's ailerons will roll the wing to the right or left.

The tail section of a glider. The fixed vertical part is the fin, and the hinged, movable piece is the rudder. On top is the fixed horizontal stabilizer. The hinged, movable section attached to it is the elevator.

A glider's tail assembly includes a fin and a rudder. The fin is a fixed vertical tail surface to which the rudder is hinged. The rudder is the hinged, vertical surface on a glider's tail that helps control direction of flight. The pilot turns the glider's nose to the left or right by moving the rudder with pedals much like the brake pedals of an automobile.

A glider's tail assembly also has a horizontal stabilizer and elevator. The horizontal stabilizer is the fixed surface attached to the top or bottom of the fin that makes a glider more stable in the air. The elevator is a hinged, horizontal surface at the glider's tail that controls how much the nose of the glider points up or down. The pilot works the elevator by moving the control stick. Finally, the pilot works the air brakes with a separate lever in the cockpit.

Most new gliders are designed to be especially lightweight. They are usually built of aluminum, fiberglass, plastics, or lightweight wood and fabric. Although gliders come in different colors, most are white because this color helps them stay cool in the heat of the sun.

There are several commonly used sailplane models. The Schweizer model 1-26 is a single-seater sailplane often flown in competition. The Schweizer

A glider crew assembles a glider. They have pulled the glider's fuselage, or body, out of the trailer and are attaching the right wing.

models 2-32 and 2-33 are used for training in the United States. These two-seater gliders have dual controls to allow the pilot to take over from the student if necessary. The pilot sits in the rear seat and the student sits in the front seat, with a great view through the canopy.

New sailplanes average between about twenty thousand and forty thousand dollars. Some people buy kits to build their own sailplane to save costs. Building a sailplane, however, is an immense job and requires a large, sheltered space. An inspector from the Federal Aviation Administration (FAA) must also examine the assembly work before the sailplane can be certified for flight.

Sailplanes are built in such a way that they can be taken apart for easier transportation. The wing halves are bolted to the body, or fuselage. The horizontal stabilizer is usually fitted onto the fuselage. And then there are various connecting cables and metal tubes to control surfaces. Typically, two people working together can assemble a glider for flight in about half an hour.

During the preflight check, the glider crew makes a careful inspection of all of the parts of the sailplane, inside and out. They examine all fittings, bolts, and cables, as well as the two-way-radio battery, oxygen, and air-pressure tubing. Special attention is given to the wingtips to be sure that they have not been damaged during previous flights. Some gliders have a small wheel mounted on a spring at the tip of each wing to protect the wingtips when the aircraft touches down.

Wingtip wheels are mounted on the wing's underside to prevent the wingtips from hitting the runway on takeoffs and landings.

Meanwhile, the pilot examines the instruments in the cockpit, including the compass, the altimeter, the airspeed indicator, and the variometer. The altimeter measures the sailplane's altitude. The airspeed indicator measures how fast the sailplane is moving forward. The variometer shows the rate at which the sailplane is gaining or losing altitude.

There are two common kinds of variometers: the dial face and pellet. A dial face variometer indicates with a needle how many feet per minute the sailplane is losing or gaining altitude. The pellet type of variometer uses two tubes with red and green balls in them. It is activated by changes in atmospheric pressure as the sailplane climbs or descends. When the green ball rises in the tube, the aircraft is gaining altitude. When the red ball rises, the plane is losing altitude.

Before takeoff, the pilot makes sure that the canopy, which is the transparent enclosure over the cockpit, is locked. Finally, with the help of a crew member, the tow release mechanism is checked.

The instrument panel of a glider. Attached to the canopy, it fits around the pilot's legs. The two red handles are used to cast off the canopy so the pilot can bail out in case of an emergency.

CHAPTER FIVE

Riding the Wind

In preparation for towing a sailplane into the air, a ground handler attaches a long, strong rope to a hook on the glider's nose.

To take off, gliders must be towed by an airplane or be pulled along by cars or winches. Winching a glider into the air is less common than towing because it does not take the glider as high and usually cannot place the aircraft directly in thermals. When a glider is being winched into the air, a winch operator attaches a cable to the glider's tow hook and reels in the cable. The cable pulls the glider forward while the pilot steers the glider upward.

Towing a glider into the air requires a powered airplane called a tow plane. Tow planes are equipped with a long polypropylene rope. The ground handler brings the end of the tow rope from the tow plane, which is at rest about 200 feet (61 m) ahead of the sailplane. When a ground handler signals "Open!" the pilot pulls a big red knob that opens a circular hook in the nose or belly of the sailplane. The ground handler then places the tow ring on the hook. When the ground handler signals "Close!" the pilot releases the knob. The ground handler tugs on the rope to check that the tow rope is hooked in place.

When all is in readiness, the ground handler signals "Ready?" If the pilot is ready, he or she will signal in the affirmative by moving an index finger in a circle. Then the person assigned to handle the wing, or the wing runner, lifts the wing of the sailplane, which has been resting on the ground. When both wings are level, the crew member at the wing signals to the tow plane pilot, who has gently

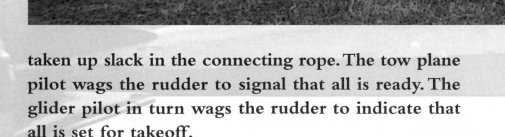

A tow plane pulls a glider down the runway. The wing runner holds the wing level until enough air is flowing over the control surfaces for the glider pilot to take off.

taken up slack in the connecting rope. The tow plane pilot wags the rudder to signal that all is ready. The glider pilot in turn wags the rudder to indicate that all is set for takeoff.

Although it is rare, a tow rope sometimes breaks. For that reason, pilots are required to practice safety procedures to carry out if the rope should break.

While the glider pilot is being towed to the proper altitude, he must keep the tow plane centered in his view out of the windshield. The pilot turns with the plane to stay below or above the wash, or air disturbance, which is caused by the tow plane's propeller. Most sailplane pilots use a high tow, which means that they fly in the smooth air above the prop wash of the tow plane.

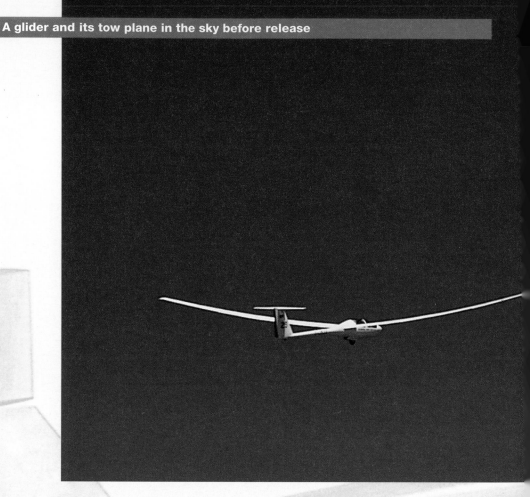

When the tow plane has towed the sailplane to the proper elevation in an area where there are thermals, the glider pilot releases the rope from the sailplane tow hook. The sailplane pilot immediately banks to the right and the tow plane pilot dives off

to the left to maximize the distance between the two. Releasing the cable from a sailplane that has taken off by winching is done similarly, except that in winching, the cable is attached to a small parachute and falls back to the ground.

It is now up to the glider pilot to maintain appropriate airspeed. The two basic maneuvers used in flying a sailplane are the straight glide and the turn. The straight glide is the easiest and requires keeping the wings level, with the optimum angle of attack, and the airspeed at the best velocity. Making a proper turn takes practice and requires using the rudder and the ailerons.

The best thermal soaring conditions are often after eleven o'clock in the morning when the sun has had a chance to heat the ground and thermals are forming. When circling in a thermal, the pilot flies at minimum sink speed to gain altitude. Experienced pilots learn to check airspeed by the sound of the air around them and the feel of the plane. An average rate of climb in a thermal is 300 feet (91 m) per minute. Thermals like these allow a sailplane to fly to 20,000 feet (6,096 m) and higher above sea level.

The pilot continually checks the yaw string, which is a 3-inch (8-cm) piece of yarn taped to the front center line of the canopy. If the yaw string streams straight back, not to the left or right, the craft is flying smoothly. The pilot also checks speed on the airspeed indicator and reads the variometer to see how fast the plane is rising or sinking.

During glider flights, thermals may quit. Sailplanes may fly out of thermals or experience sink, causing them to land in unexpected places. When sailplanes land somewhere other than an airport or gliderport, the glider pilot radios to a ground crew or gets to a phone to call for assistance after landing. The crew comes with a specially fitted trailer, takes apart and packs the glider on the trailer, and drives back to the gliderport.

Low clouds have forced this pilot to land his sailplane in a pasture. A helper has arrived with a trailer in tow to carry craft and pilot back to the gliderport.

CAUTION WANDERING STOCK

Weather is a vital factor in soaring. Low pressure, for example, because it brings rain and reduces thermals, makes for poor flying conditions. As long as there is good visibility, an experienced glider pilot can recognize different types of clouds in the sky, which helps in forecasting weather conditions. Glider pilots also learn to recognize various updrafts, including ridge winds, mountain lee waves, and, of course, thermals.

Ridge lift is found when a breeze of 10 to 20 miles (16 to 32 km) an hour blows squarely up a hill and over the crest. Ridge winds are found on many ocean-side cliffs. One famous ridge is located along the Allegheny Mountains in the eastern United States.

When ridge running, or ridge soaring, pilots usually fly only about 100 to 200 feet (30 to 61 m) above the ridge. The pilot must be careful not to stray too far to the lee, or downwind, side because the air can tumble down quickly and cause considerable turbulence and loss of lift.

Some experienced pilots also enjoy what is called wave soaring on mountain lee waves. Such lee waves, like those that form on the eastern side of the

Mountain lee waves perfect for soaring are found alongside mountains around the world, including Mount Cook on New Zealand's South Island.

Sierra Nevada Mountains in California and on the Continental Divide, offer great wave soaring. By staying near the upwind edge of the wave, a warmly dressed pilot with an oxygen supply can climb to 30,000 feet (9,144 m) and more.

CHAPTER SIX

Soaring Solo

You don't have to take the pilot's seat to experience the joys of soaring, but it might be more fun!

To become a licensed glider pilot, students must be fourteen years of age or older, though they may begin ground instruction at a younger age. There is no cost for the student license, which is valid for two years and renewable. No physical examination is required, but students have to certify that they have no health problems that would interfere with piloting a sailplane.

A flight in a two-seat trainer ship is a good introduction to the world of soaring. The pilot will answer questions and may even let passengers take over the controls for a few minutes to get the feel of soaring.

There are many certified glider flying schools in the United States. Before signing up with a school, possible students need to collect lots of information. How long does it take to complete the course? What are the costs? Is there a package plan that will take beginners all the way to a license? Is the instructor's time and the fee for the tow plane included in the quoted rate?

Some people find it more inexpensive and social to join a soaring club. Some clubs own planes that members can use for modest fees and offer instruction at fairly low rates. Members, however, are expected to help around the field. Such clubs, large and small, are found in most states of the United States as well as in Canada, South America, Europe, Australia, New Zealand, and Asia.

Classroom instruction is an important part of becoming a glider pilot. Here, Doris Grove, a holder of many world glider records, explains how to fly the traffic pattern.

Student pilots learn about glider parts and how they work and how to handle a glider on the ground. They also learn airport rules, landing patterns, and FAA glider regulations. Soaring, however, is a sport that must be learned through hands-on experience.

After completing ground-school training, student pilots are issued a student glider pilot certificate by the FAA. Student pilots may then begin flight training with qualified instructors, which includes

learning how to operate controls, how to maneuver gliders, and what to do in emergencies. Students keep a log of all flying time, which the instructor endorses with his or her license number issued by the FAA.

When a student pilot is ready, usually after at least a dozen flights with an instructor, he or she takes an oral exam. When the instructor approves, the student pilot may take a solo flight. The completion of a student's first solo flight is often cele-

47

brated by a traditional ceremony in which a crew member cuts off the new pilot's shirttails and presents them to him or her. Many pilots save this memento for a lifetime.

After soloing, pilots can begin to work toward a private pilot license. To get this license, pilots must be at least sixteen years old, have made more than thirty flights (including seven or more hours of solo time), pass a written examination, and be flight-tested by an FAA-approved examiner.

Private pilots can carry nonpaying passengers on pleasure trips. To carry a paying passenger requires a commercial pilot's license, which takes still more training. The minimum age required to try for a commercial license is eighteen.

The long-distance cross-country trips that pilots with private and commercial pilot licenses take require lots of planning. Pilots must study aeronautical maps and charts of the proposed course and identify landmarks. Throughout the flight, they have to check weather reports by radio frequently.

And finally, some pilots study for a flight instructor certificate. Such a certificate is required to give flight instruction in sailplanes.

CHAPTER SEVEN

Gliding for Gold

A contestant in the World Gliding Championships streaks in for a landing, dumping water weights carried in tanks in the wings.

Some ambitious glider pilots take part in competitions. In some events, participants compete against themselves to accomplish individual goals. In other events, participants compete against other pilots.

Every two years, the International Gliding Commission sanctions an international competition open to soaring pilots from around the world called the World Gliding Championships. The Fédération Aéronautique Internationale (FAI), founded in 1905 and headquartered in Paris, oversees the competition. No matter which country a pilot is from, the same tasks and proof of achievement are required to earn an FAI badge.

Although different countries host this international event, it has been held in the United States several times. The first championship held in the United States was hosted in Marfa, Texas, in 1970. In 1983, the competition was in Hobbs, New Mexico, and in 1991, in Uvalde, Texas.

The Soaring Society of America (SSA), founded in 1932 by a small group of pilots, sanctions five national championship events yearly and more than fifteen regional events. The SSA also administers awards for soaring achievements in the United States.

The most basic glider awards are the A, B, and C badges. All of the badges are circular lapel pins with white gulls on a blue background. The A badge (with one gull) is awarded for completing a solo flight and passing an oral exam on FAA glider regulations. The B badge (with two gulls) is awarded for completing a thirty-minute flight. The C badge (with three gulls) is awarded for completing a sixty-minute flight.

More experienced pilots can try for the silver badge and the gold badge. Up to three diamonds can be worn with either badge. A silver badge is awarded for completing a duration flight of at least five hours, a distance flight of at least 31.1 miles (50 km),

Before a contest begins, crews position gliders on the grid. Tow planes will tow the gliders into the air to start their tasks.

and an altitude flight with a gain in height of at least 3,281 feet (1,000 m). A gold badge is awarded for completing a duration flight of at least five hours, a distance flight of at least 186.4 miles (300 km), and an altitude flight with a gain in height of at least 9,842 feet (3,000 m).

Only a few soaring pilots earn the gold badge or the diamonds. One diamond is added for each of the following three achievements: a distance flight of at least 310.7 miles (500 km), a flight of at least 186.4 miles (300 km) to a declared destination, and an altitude flight with a gain in height of at least 16,405 feet (5,000 m).

All award candidates must fill out application forms for the Soaring Society of America (SSA). Such achievements must be confirmed by an SSA observer and aerial photographs and readings taken in the sailplane as proof of altitude gain and distance flown.

Glider pilots are constantly setting new and astonishing soaring records. Sailplanes have stayed aloft for sixty hours, climbed to an altitude of almost 50,000 feet (15,240 m), and flown for more than 900 miles (1,448 km) in a straight flight.

In SSA contests held throughout the United States, pilots can enter in various classes. In Open Class, for example, sailplanes can have unlimited wingspans, while in Standard Class, the wingspans can measure only 49 feet (15 m) and the use of wing flaps is not permitted. In such contests, pilots fly triangular courses of various lengths, sometimes as far as 300 miles (483 km).

Soaring is not without risk, but the number of casualties from the sport each year is low. Statistics show that soaring is safer than driving a car. One important factor in the safety of gliders is that there is no fuel to ignite during a crash landing.

Gliders also provide the scientific community with valuable information. For example, the National Center for Atmospheric Research regularly launches a glider with a mounted camera to gather weather and atmospheric data.

Even in this age of transcontinental flights, supersonic jets, and space launches, the sport of soaring continues to flourish. If you would like to glide on the air and look down at the world from the sky, you too can join this growing community of soaring enthusiasts.

After release during a competition, gliders circle in a thermal, waiting to fly out on course. The group resembles a flock of birds and, in fact, is called a gaggle.

Soaring Terms

aileron—the movable panel at the rear edge of each of a glider's wingtips used to help turn the glider

airspeed indicator—an instrument used to measure how fast the glider is moving forward

altimeter—an instrument used to measure altitude

canopy—the transparent enclosure over the cockpit

drag—wind resistance to the glider's forward motion

elevator—the hinged, horizontal surface at the glider's tail that controls how much the glider's nose points up or down

fin—the fixed vertical tail surface to which the rudder is hinged

flaps—hinged panels at the rear edge of a glider's wings used to help with the glider's handling at low speeds

fuselage—the body of an aircraft

horizontal stabilizer—the fixed surface attached to the top or bottom of the fin that makes a glider more stable in the air

lift—the upward force that allows a glider to fly

rudder—the hinged, vertical surface on a glider's tail used to help control direction of flight

thermal—a column of rising warm air

variometer—a vertical-speed indicator that measures the rate of climb or descent

yaw string—the short piece of string attached to a glider's canopy that streams straight back with the wind when the glider is in a normal line of flight

Organizations and Publications

ORGANIZATIONS

The Soaring Society of America
P.O. Box E
Hobbs, NM 88241-7504

National Soaring Museum
51 Soaring Hill Drive
Elmira, NY 14903

BOOKS

Ayres, Carter A. *Soaring*. Minneapolis: Lerner Publications, 1985.

Berliner, Don. *Before the Wright Brothers.* Minneapolis: Lerner Publications, 1990.

Conway, Carle. *Joy of Soaring.* Hobbs, N. Mex.: Soaring Society of America, 1989.

Coombs, Charles. *Soaring: Where Hawks and Eagles Fly.* New York: Henry Holt, 1988.

Jennings, Terry. *Planes, Gliders, Helicopters and Other Flying Machines.* New York: Kingfisher, 1993.

MAGAZINES

Soaring
P.O. Box E
Hobbs, NM 88241–7504

You may also subscribe to the British Gliding Association magazine *Sailplane & Gliding* through the Soaring Society of America.

Resources on the Internet

Due to the changeable nature of the Internet, sites can appear and disappear quickly. Here are a couple of resources that provided useful information on soaring at the time of publication. (Please note that Web addresses must be entered with capital and lowercase letters exactly as they are shown.)

- **The Soaring Society of America (SSA) has a World Wide Web page that provides general soaring information and links to other soaring Web sites at the following address:**
  http://acro.harvard.edu/SSA/ssa_homepg.html

- **The Fédération Aéronautique Internationale (FAI) has a World Wide Web page that provides the latest aviation news and world records at the following address:**
  http://www.fai.org/~fai/

Index

Page numbers in *italics* indicate illustrations.

About the Author

Phyllis J. Perry has written over thirty books for teachers and young people, including *Ballooning*, *The Snow Cats*, *The Crocodilians: Reminders of the Age of Dinosaurs*, *The Fiddlehoppers: Crickets, Katydids, and Locusts*, and *Sea Stars and Dragons* for Franklin Watts. She received her doctorate in curriculum and instruction from the University of Colorado. Dr. Perry lives with her husband, David, in Boulder, Colorado.